CRANFORD

In Cranford nobody is very rich, but you must not talk about being poor. Indeed not! That would be a very vulgar thing to do. And in Cranford it is important not to be vulgar. At the Honourable Mrs Jamieson's evening parties there is only thin bread-and-butter (expensive food would be vulgar), and Miss Deborah Jenkyns is extremely cross when Miss Jessie Brown talks openly about her shopkeeper uncle. An uncle in trade! What horror!

The rules of society were different 150 years ago, but people stay the same. The ladies of Cranford are just like people in any age. They can be sad, happy, proud, brave, angry, jealous – and very kind. When dear, gentle Miss Matty is in trouble, everybody wants to help her. And though there are many sadnesses in Miss Matty's life, there is also a very happy surprise waiting for her . . .

OXFORD BOOKWORMS LIBRARY
Classics

Cranford

Stage 4 (1400 headwords)

Series Editor: Jennifer Bassett
Founder Editor: Tricia Hedge
Activities Editors: Jennifer Bassett and Christine Lindop

ELIZABETH GASKELL

Cranford

Retold by
Kate Mattock

OXFORD UNIVERSITY PRESS

OXFORD
UNIVERSITY PRESS

Great Clarendon Street, Oxford OX2 6DP

Oxford University Press is a department of the University of Oxford.
It furthers the University's objective of excellence in research, scholarship,
and education by publishing worldwide in

Oxford New York

Auckland Cape Town Dar es Salaam Hong Kong Karachi
Kuala Lumpur Madrid Melbourne Mexico City Nairobi
New Delhi Shanghai Taipei Toronto

With offices in

Argentina Austria Brazil Chile Czech Republic France Greece
Guatemala Hungary Italy Japan Poland Portugal Singapore
South Korea Switzerland Thailand Turkey Ukraine Vietnam

ISBN 978 0 19 479167 0

Printed in Spain

ACKNOWLEDGEMENTS
Illustrated by: John Holder

Word count (main text): 15,015 words

For more information on the Oxford Bookworms Library,
visit www.oup.com/elt/bookworms

CONTENTS

CONTENTS

1

Our society

The first thing to say is that Cranford is held by the ladies. They rent all the best houses. If a married couple comes to live in the town, the gentleman soon disappears from sight. He is either frightened away by being the only man at the Cranford evening parties or he is at his business all week in Drumble, twenty miles away by train.

Anyway, what is there for a gentleman to do in Cranford? The town already has a doctor, and the ladies manage everything else perfectly well themselves. They keep the gardens tidy and their maid-servants busy. They have opinions on every important matter without troubling themselves with unnecessary reasons or arguments. They know exactly what everyone in the town is doing. They are kind to the poor and, usually, very kind and friendly to each other.

'A man,' as one of them said to me once, 'is *terribly* in the way in the house!'

The Cranford ladies are not fashionable, and they prefer the old ways. When I lived there, they had exact rules for visiting, which they explained most seriously to any young people who came to stay: 'Our friends have asked how you are, my dear, after your journey. They are sure to call on you the day after tomorrow, so be ready to receive them from twelve o'clock. From twelve to three are our calling hours.'

Then, after the friends had called: 'Always return a call within three days, my dear. And never stay longer than a quarter of an hour.'

The result of this rule, of course, was that nothing interesting was ever discussed. We talked about things like the weather, and left at the right time.

One or two of the Cranford ladies were poor, I imagine, but they tried to hide it, and the others kindly helped. When Mrs Forrester gave a party and her little maid had to get the tea-tray from under the sofa on which we sat, everyone just went on talking. And when Mrs Forrester pretended she did not know what cakes were on the tray, no one looked surprised. But we knew, and she knew that we knew, and we knew that she knew that we knew, that she had made the cakes herself that morning.

In fact, the Cranfordians thought it was 'vulgar' (a favourite word) to give anything expensive to eat or drink at their evening parties. Thin bread-and-butter was all that the Honourable Mrs Jamieson gave – and *she* was related to the late Lord Glenmire.

Yes, spending money was always 'vulgar', and we certainly did not tell anyone that we had very little to spend. So I shall never forget the horror when an old army captain came to live in Cranford and spoke openly about being poor! In the street! The ladies were already rather cross about the arrival of a gentleman, and even more cross that he was going to work for a new railway near the town. If, as well as being a man and working for that awful railway, Captain Brown was going to talk about being poor, *then nobody must speak to him.*

*The little maid had to get the tea-tray
from under the sofa.*

I was surprised, therefore, when I visited the town a year after the captain arrived, to discover that he had made himself very popular. My own friends had been strongly against calling on him, but now they welcomed him into their house, even before twelve o'clock in the morning. He had been friendly and sensible, though the Cranford ladies had been cool, and at last his helpfulness had won him a place in their hearts.

Captain Brown was living, with his two daughters, in a small house on the edge of the town. He was probably over sixty at this time, though he looked younger. In fact, Miss Brown, his elder daughter, looked almost as old as he did. She was only about forty, but her face was white and tired.

Miss Jessie Brown was ten years younger and twenty times prettier. Her face was round and had dimples. Miss Jenkyns once said, when she was annoyed with Captain Brown (for a reason I'll explain later), that it was time Miss Jessie stopped having dimples and looking like a child. There was indeed something childish about the way she looked, but I liked her face. So did everybody – and I do not think she could prevent the dimples.

I first saw the Brown family together in Cranford church. The captain sang loudly and happily; and when we came out, he smiled at everyone and patiently helped Miss Brown with her umbrella.

I wondered what the Cranford ladies did with him at their card-parties. We had often been glad in the past that there were no gentlemen to worry about. Indeed, we had almost persuaded ourselves that it was 'vulgar' to be a man. So now, when Miss Deborah Jenkyns (with whom I was staying) gave a party for me and invited the Browns, I wondered how the evening would go.

It was the third week of November, so it was dark by four o'clock. The card-tables were arranged. Candles and clean packs of cards were put on each one. The fire was lit. The maid was given final orders. And there we stood in our best dresses, ready to light the candles as soon as the first person knocked at the door.

The Browns arrived when the tea-trays were on the tables. The captain took immediate care of all the ladies, passing round cups and bread-and-butter. He was clearly a favourite. But all the time he kept an eye on his elder daughter – a sick woman, I was sure. Miss Jessie seemed almost as popular as her father. She talked to those not playing cards, and later she sang while Miss Jenkyns beat time to the music.

It was good of Miss Jenkyns to do this, because she had been much annoyed by Miss Jessie a little earlier. 'My mother's brother,' Miss Jessie had said to Miss Pole, 'is a shopkeeper in Edinburgh.' An uncle in trade! Oh dear! The Honourable Mrs Jamieson was sitting at the nearest card-table and Miss Jenkyns had coughed loudly to prevent her hearing the terrible words. But Miss Jessie had happily repeated them, telling Miss Pole that her uncle sold the best knitting-wool in Edinburgh. So, I say again, it was good of Miss Jenkyns to beat time to her song.

At a quarter to nine, when the trays came back with a

little more food, there was conversation. After a while Captain Brown began to talk about books.

'Have you seen any of *The Pickwick Papers*?' he asked. (It was 1836, and Mr Dickens's new book was appearing month by month.)

'Yes, I have,' answered Miss Jenkyns. Miss Jenkyns was the daughter of a past rector of Cranford church and, having his library of church books and sermons, she considered that she knew about books of all kinds.

'And what do you think of them?' asked the captain enthusiastically. 'Aren't they good?'

'Not as good as Dr Johnson,' replied Miss Jenkyns. 'But perhaps your man is young. If he copies the style of the great doctor, he may succeed.'

'But it's quite a different thing, my dear madam!' cried Captain Brown. 'Let me just read you something from this month's paper.'

The *Pickwick* story he read was a very amusing one about a party in Bath, but Miss Jenkyns did not smile. She sent me to fetch Dr Johnson's *Rasselas*, and read us a slow conversation, full of long words, between Rasselas and his teacher.

'Now you understand,' she said grandly as she put the book down, 'why I prefer Dr Johnson as a writer. Beginners should copy his style. I did, when I began to write letters. Your favourite should do the same.'

'I hope he won't copy anything so self-important!' said Captain Brown.

6

He was sorry later for what he had said, and stood near Miss Jenkyns's armchair, trying to please her. But she did not give in. The next day she said what she thought of Miss Jessie's dimples.

2

The captain

It was impossible to live in Cranford for a month and not know everybody's daily habits. So, long before my visit ended, I knew a lot about the Browns. They were indeed poor. And the captain was extraordinarily kind. One Sunday morning after church, he met a poor old woman who was fetching her dinner from the town bakehouse. The street was wet and she was rather shaky on her legs, so the captain carried her baked meat and potatoes home for her! Cranford people did not do this kind of thing, but the captain was not at all ashamed of himself.

Miss Jenkyns could not forgive Captain Brown for his unkind opinion of Dr Johnson, so I did not see much of the family until I went on to stay with Miss Pole. I learnt then that Miss Brown was seriously ill. And when I saw how difficult she was, and how endlessly kind her father and sister were to her, I understood a little better and forgave Miss Jessie for her childish way of dressing.

The captain tried hard to make peace with Miss Jenkyns, but she remained cool. No gentleman, surely, could prefer Mr Dickens to Dr Johnson!

That was the situation when I left Cranford to return to my father in Drumble. But several of the ladies sent me news of the dear little town. Miss Pole wrote, asking for some knitting-wool. Miss Matty Jenkyns (Miss Deborah's younger sister) wrote nice, kind, disorganized letters, occasionally giving her own opinion but more often giving her elder sister's. And Miss Deborah Jenkyns herself wrote – grand, slow-moving letters, using words like 'Brunonian' for 'Brown'.

My next visit to Cranford was in the summer. No one had been born or married since I was last there, and no one had died. Everyone lived in the same house and wore the same unfashionable clothes. The greatest excitement was that the Misses Jenkyns had bought a new carpet. Oh, what busy work Miss Matty and I had in the afternoons, covering it with newspaper where the sun shone in!

Captain Brown and Miss Jenkyns were still not very friendly. Miss Jenkyns always talked *at* the captain and, though he did not reply, he made it quite clear that he preferred the writings of Mr Dickens to those of Dr Johnson. Indeed, he used to read Mr Dickens's books while walking through the streets, and was so deeply interested in his reading that once he nearly knocked Miss Jenkyns down.

The poor, brave captain! His clothes looked very old and worn, but he seemed as bright as ever, unless he was asked about his elder daughter's health. 'She's in great pain,' he replied, 'though we do what we can.'

Miss Matty told me that, in fact, he and his younger daughter had done everything possible to make the patient

What busy work Miss Matty and I had in the afternoons!

comfortable, whatever the cost. 'And Miss Jessie's a wonderful nurse. My dear, if you saw her as I have, you'd never laugh again at her childish pink ribbons.'

I felt ashamed and spoke to Miss Jessie with twice as much respect next time we met. She looked exhausted, but she pushed back the tears in her pretty eyes. 'What a good town Cranford is!' she said. 'Everyone sends my sister presents.'

Captain Brown called one day to thank Miss Jenkyns for many little kindnesses I had not known about. He had suddenly become like an old man, and his deep voice trembled when he spoke about his elder daughter. 'There is no hope,' he said. 'Thank God we have Jessie!' Then he quickly shook everyone's hand and left the room.

That afternoon, we saw little groups in the street, all listening with horror to some story. Miss Jenkyns sent out Jenny the maid, who came back in tears. 'Oh, Miss Jenkyns! Captain Brown has been killed by that cruel railway!'

'How? Where, where?' Miss Matty ran out into the street and brought back the man who was telling the story. 'Oh, say it's not true!' Miss Matty cried.

The man stood there with his wet boots on the new carpet and no one noticed. 'It's true, Miss,' he said. 'I saw it myself. The captain was reading some new book while he waited for the down-train. Then he looked up suddenly and saw a little girl on the railway line, just as the train was coming into the station. He ran forwards and caught her, but then he fell and the train went straight over him. The child's safe, though.

The poor captain would be glad of that, Miss, wouldn't he?'

Miss Jenkyns's face was very white. 'Matilda, bring me my bonnet,' she commanded Miss Matty. 'I must go to those girls . . . God forgive me if I ever spoke sharply to the captain!'

When she came back, she did not want to talk much. Mr Hoggins, the Cranford doctor, had said that Miss Brown would not live for many more days. Miss Jessie did not want her sister to hear the terrible news of her father's death, so Miss Brown was told that her father had been called away on railway business.

Next day, the newspaper had the full story of the accident. 'The brave gentleman,' it said, 'was reading this month's *Pickwick Papers.*'

'Poor, dear, silly man!' Miss Jenkyns shook her head, and busily sewed some black ribbon on her bonnet for the funeral.

She went with Miss Jessie to the funeral, while Miss Pole, Miss Matty and I sat with Miss Brown.

Next day when we returned, we could see that Miss Brown was dying.

'Oh, Jessie!' she whispered. 'How selfish I've been! God forgive me!'

'Sssh, love, sssh!' said Miss Jessie in tears.

'And my dear, dear father! He can never know now how I loved him.'

'He does know, dearest. He . . . he has gone before you to his resting-place. He knows now how you loved him.' The tears ran like rain down Miss Jessie's face. A few moments later her sister lay calm and quiet.

11

After this second funeral, Miss Jenkyns made Miss Jessie stay with us. Miss Jessie had only about £20 a year to live on, and one day she and I began to discuss how she could earn some money.

'I can sew,' said Jessie, 'and I like nursing . . .'

Suddenly Miss Jenkyns entered the room in unusual excitement. 'My dear Miss Jessie! Such a surprise! There is a gentleman downstairs whom you once knew—'

Miss Jessie went white, then red.

'—a gentleman, my dear, who wants to know if you will see him.'

'Is it . . .? It isn't . . .?' Miss Jessie could not finish.

'This is his visiting-card,' said Miss Jenkyns. She gave the card to Miss Jessie and made a strange face at me over her head. 'May he come up?'

'Oh, oh yes!' said Miss Jessie. She picked up some of Miss Matty's knitting and began to be very busy.

Miss Jenkyns rang the bell. 'Bring Captain Gordon upstairs,' she told the maid.

A tall, fine, sincere-looking man of about forty walked in. He shook hands with Miss Jessie, who looked down at the floor.

Miss Jenkyns asked me to come downstairs and help her prepare some fruit. Although Miss Jessie tried to make me stay, I could not refuse to help Miss Jenkyns. Instead of preparing fruit, however, Miss Jenkyns told me what Captain Gordon had told her. He had been in the army with Captain Brown and had fallen in love with Jessie when she was only eighteen. When he had inherited an estate in Scotland, he had asked her to marry him – and she had refused in order to nurse her sister. Gordon had then gone angrily abroad. He was in Rome when he saw the report of Captain Brown's death.

Just then Miss Matty, who had been out all the morning, happened to come home. 'Deborah!' she cried. 'There's a gentleman upstairs with his arm round Miss Jessie's waist!' Miss Matty's eyes were large with horror.

Miss Jenkyns's reply surprised her sister greatly.

'The best place in the world for his arm to be in. Go away, Matilda, and mind your own business.'

The last time I ever saw Miss Jenkyns was years after this. She and Miss Matty and Miss Pole had all visited Miss Jessie (now Mrs Gordon) in Scotland and returned with wonderful stories of her home, her husband and her pretty dimples. Now, at the time I am speaking of, Miss Jenkyns had grown old. Miss Jessie's daughter, little Flora Gordon, had come down to Cranford on a visit. When I came in, Miss Jenkyns was lying on the sofa and Flora was reading aloud to her.

'Ah, my dear!' Miss Jenkyns said to me. 'I cannot see as well as I used to. Did you ever read *Rasselas?* It's a wonderful book – wonderful! And so good for Flora. Much better than that strange book by Mr Dickens that killed poor Captain Brown . . .'

3

A love-affair of long ago

After Miss Jenkyns's death, I did not expect to go to Cranford again. It was pleasant, therefore, to receive a letter from Miss Pole, inviting me to stay, and then a few days later a letter from Miss Matty, also inviting me. I promised to go to Miss Matty as soon as I had ended my visit to Miss Pole; and I went to see her the day after my arrival in Cranford. Miss Matty began to cry as soon as she saw me.

I took her hand, feeling very sorry for her, all alone in the world without her sister. 'Dear Miss Matty!' said I.

'My dear, I'd rather you didn't call me Matty. *She* didn't like it. Please, my love, will you call me Matilda?'

I promised – and I did try. We all tried, but with so little success that in the end we called her 'Miss Matty' again.

My visit to Miss Pole was very quiet. The Honourable Mrs Jamieson was too fat and lazy to give many parties and, without Miss Jenkyns to lead them, the other ladies did not quite know what to do. So I sewed my father's shirts, while Miss Pole did her knitting and told me stories about Cranford. One of her stories was about a love-affair she had suspected many years before.

After a week, I moved to Miss Matilda's house. How anxious she was about everything! 'Is your room all right,

14

dear?' she said worriedly as I unpacked. 'The fire's not very bright. My sister used to arrange things so well. She could train a servant in a week, but Fanny's been with me for four months . . .'

Maid-servants were always a problem to the ladies of Cranford, and specially to poor Miss Matilda. There were not many gentlemen in the town, as I have said, but the number of handsome young working men was alarming. Sometimes they had to call at the house. What would happen if the maid fell in love with one of them? Pretty Fanny was not allowed to have any 'followers', but her mistress suspected that she had very many – and I myself once saw something strangely like a young man hiding behind the kitchen clock.

However, during my visit Fanny had to leave; and I agreed to stay and help Miss Matilda with the new maid. Martha was a rough, honest-looking girl from a farm. I liked her, and I promised to teach her the rules of the house. These rules were, of course, Miss Jenkyns's rules. Miss Matilda had whispered against many of them during her sister's life, but now they must stay. About that, she was certain. About everything else, she was anxious and undecided.

And now I come to the love-affair. It seems that Miss Pole had a cousin who, long ago, had asked Miss Matilda to marry him. His name was Thomas Holbrook and he lived a few miles from Cranford on his own estate, called Woodley. He was a real country-man, very open and sincere, Miss Pole told me. 'He reads aloud,' she added, 'more beautifully than anyone I have ever heard, except Mr Jenkyns, the late rector.'

'Why didn't Miss Matilda marry him?' I asked.

'Perhaps the rector and Miss Jenkyns didn't think cousin Thomas was enough of a gentleman for her. You know the Jenkynses are related in some way to Sir Peter Arley. Miss Jenkyns was very proud of that.'

*I once saw something strangely like a young man
hiding behind the kitchen clock.*

'Poor Miss Matty! Has she ever seen Mr Holbrook since?'

'I don't think she has. He stopped coming into Cranford after she refused him.'

'And how old is he now?'

'About seventy, my dear,' said Miss Pole.

Soon after this, strangely enough, I saw Mr Holbrook. Miss Matilda and I were looking at some coloured silks that had arrived at Mr Johnson's shop in High Street, when a tall, thin old man in country clothes hurried in. He waited impatiently, then told the shop-boy what he wanted. Miss Matilda heard his voice, and suddenly sat down. At once, I guessed who it was.

'Miss Jenkyns wants the black silk,' another shop-boy called across the shop.

Mr Holbrook heard the name. 'Matty – Miss Matilda! I didn't recognize you! How are you?' He shook her hand warmly. 'I didn't recognize you!' he repeated.

We left the shop without buying anything and Mr Holbrook walked home with us. He was clearly delighted to meet his old love again. He even spoke of Miss Jenkyns as 'Your poor sister! Well, well! We all have our faults.' And he said as he left us that he hoped to see Miss Matty again soon.

She went straight to her room. When she came down at tea-time, I saw that she had been crying.

❧❧

A few days later, a note came from Mr Holbrook. It was now June. Would Miss Matty and I like to come out to Woodley for a day? he asked. He had also invited his cousin

Miss Pole, so the three of us could ride in the same carriage.

At first, Miss Matty refused to accept. Then, when we finally persuaded her, she went back to the shop and chose a new bonnet for the visit.

It was clear that she had never been to Woodley before. She trembled as we drove there, and I could see that she was thinking about the past. Towards the end of the journey, she sat very straight and looked sadly out of the carriage windows.

The house itself stood among fields, and there was an old garden full of roses and little fruit-trees. 'It's very pretty,' whispered Miss Matty as Mr Holbrook appeared at the door, smiling warmly.

The day passed very happily. We sat and talked in a nice, untidy room filled with books. I asked to look at the garden, and this pleased the old gentleman. His housekeeper gave us dinner in a kind of kitchen, and later I walked with him across his fields. Then, when we came back to the house, he offered to read us some new poems by Mr Tennyson.

'Yes, please do, cousin Thomas!' said Miss Pole.

I thought this was because she wanted me to hear his beautiful reading. Afterwards, though, she said it was because she had wanted to go on with her knitting.

Whatever Mr Holbrook did was agreeable to Miss Matty. She fell asleep soon after he began a long poem called *Locksley Hall*, but she woke up when his voice stopped. 'How pretty!' she said quickly.

'Pretty, madam? It's beautiful!'

The poem was about lost love, but Miss Matty had not

Mr Holbrook appeared at the door, smiling warmly.

heard it. 'Oh, yes, I meant beautiful!' she apologized. 'It's so like that beautiful poem by Dr Johnson that my sister used to read. I forget the name of it.'

'Which poem do you mean, madam? What was it about?'

'I don't remember what it was about. But it was by Dr Johnson and it was very beautiful . . .'

As we got into the carriage to return to Cranford, Mr Holbrook promised to call on us soon. This seemed to please Miss Matty, although as soon as we had left Woodley, she began to worry about Martha. Had the girl had a 'follower' while we were absent?

However, there was no sign of a 'follower' as Martha came to help us out of the carriage. She always took good care of Miss Matty, and tonight she said:

'Eh! Dear madam, you shouldn't go out in the evening in such a thin shawl! You'll catch cold, and at your age, madam, you should be careful.'

'My age!' said Miss Matty, speaking almost crossly. 'My age! Why, Martha, how old do you think I am?'

'Well, madam, I'd say you were getting close to sixty – but I didn't mean any harm.'

'Martha, I'm not yet fifty-two!' said Miss Matty. Today's visit had reminded her of the past, and I think she did not want to remember how long ago it was.

Miss Matty said nothing to me, then or ever, about Mr Holbrook but, by careful watching, I saw that she still loved him. She now wore her best cap every day, and sat near the window to see down into the street.

He came. He asked politely about our journey home from Woodley, then suddenly he got up. 'Well, madam,' he said to Miss Matilda, 'can I bring you anything from Paris? I'm going there in a week or two.'

'To Paris?!'

'Yes. I've always wished to see it . . . Oh dear, I almost forgot! Here are the poems you liked at my house.' He pulled a small packet from his coat-pocket and gave it to her. 'Goodbye, Matty,' he said. 'Take care of yourself.'

He had gone. But he had given her a book and he had called her Matty, just as he used to thirty years ago.

───◈───

Soon after this I left Cranford, ordering Martha to take good care of her mistress and to write to me if anything was wrong.

In November, she sent me a note to say that Miss Matilda was 'very low and not eating her food', so I went back. Miss Matty certainly looked white and miserable. I called on Miss Pole next morning and learnt that Thomas Holbrook was seriously ill. The journey to Paris had been too much for him. Ah! So that was why Miss Matty was miserable.

'I must come back with you, my dear,' said Miss Pole, 'because I promised to give Miss Matty the latest report on cousin Thomas. I'm sorry to say his housekeeper has informed me that he'll not live much longer.'

I took Miss Pole into Miss Matty's little drawing-room and left the two ladies alone.

Miss Matty did not come down to dinner, but that evening she talked to me about her girlhood. Clearly, she had been thinking about her sister, who had not wanted her to marry Thomas Holbrook. Perhaps they had not been kind thoughts, and now Miss Matty felt sorry, because she wanted to tell me how good and how clever Deborah had been. She and her mother had taught cooking and sewing to poor girls, and she had once danced with a lord, and she used to go to Arley Hall where they kept thirty servants . . . Deborah had also nursed her through a long illness. That illness, I decided, had followed Miss Matty's refusal of Mr Holbrook.

The next day, Miss Pole came to say that Mr Holbrook was dead. Miss Matty trembled and could not speak. She remained silent all that evening. Then she called the maid.

'Martha,' she said at last, 'you are young . . .'

Martha curtsied. 'Yes, madam. Twenty-two.'

'I did say that you must not have any followers. But perhaps, Martha, you will one day meet a young man whom you like and who likes you. If you do, and if I decide that he is respectable, he may come to see you once a week.'

Miss Matty was surprised, very surprised, by Martha's ready answer. 'Please, madam, there's Jem Hearn, madam. He earns three-and-sixpence a day, and he's six feet tall, and he'll be glad to come tomorrow night!'

4

Poor Peter

I have often noticed that everyone has some little meanness.
Miss Matty Jenkyns was mean about candles. In the
winter afternoons, she used to knit for hours just by firelight;
and though candles were brought in with our tea, we never
burnt more than one of them.

One evening, I remember, this meanness quite annoyed
me. Miss Matty had fallen asleep and it was too dark for me
to sew even in front of the fire. When Martha brought in the
lighted candle and tea, Miss Matty woke up with a sad little
jump. She had been dreaming about her early life, I think,
because all through tea she talked about her childhood.
Then, afterwards, she went to her room to fetch some old
family letters. I wanted more light by which to read them,
but Miss Matty still refused to light a second candle.

The earliest letters were two yellow packets, tied together.
'Letters between my dear parents before their marriage in
July 1774,' said Miss Jenkyns's writing. The rector of
Cranford was about twenty-seven at that time, and Miss
Matty's mother was not yet eighteen. The only writing of the
rector's I had seen before was a grand sermon in the style of
Dr Johnson. So it was strange to read these fresh young
letters from him, full of love for his Molly. The girl's letters

23

were rather different – all about wedding clothes, and a white silk dress she desperately wanted.

'We must burn them, I think,' said Miss Matty doubtfully. 'No one will care for them when I've gone.' One by one, she dropped the letters into the fire. The room was light enough now.

The other letters were written between about 1775 and 1805. There were sweet letters between the mother and grandmother when Deborah was born. There were later letters from the rector, full of Latin words. There were badly-spelt replies from his wife about *'bewtiful little Matty'*. And there was one letter from the grandfather about a son. How strange, I thought, that I had never heard of this son before.

Then we came to Miss Jenkyns's letters. It took us two nights to read them all. The longest ones were written during a visit to Newcastle-upon-Tyne early in 1805. Some people were expecting Napoleon Buonaparte to land there, and Miss Jenkyns was clearly alarmed.

'It was a frightening time, my dear,' explained Miss Matty. 'I used to wake up at night and think I heard the French entering Cranford! My father, I remember, wrote a lot of sermons against Napoleon.'

The son, Peter Arley Jenkyns ('poor Peter!' Miss Matty began to call him), was at school at Shrewsbury by this time. The rector wrote in Latin to his boy, and the boy wrote back careful 'show' letters, with notes to his mother at the end: *'Mother dear, do send me a cake!'*

Soon, 'poor Peter' was in trouble at school. There were

One by one, Miss Matty dropped the letters into the fire.

letters to his father apologizing for some wrong-doing, and a note to his mother. '*My dearest Mother, I will be a better boy. I will, indeed. But please don't be ill because of me. I'm not worth it.*'

After this note, Miss Matty was crying too much to speak. She got up and took it to her room in case it was burnt by mistake. 'Poor Peter!' she said. 'He was always in trouble. He was too fond of fun and jokes. Poor Peter!'

Peter won no honours at school, it seemed, and he was brought back to Cranford, to study at home.

'He was a kind boy in many ways,' said Miss Matty. 'Like dear Captain Brown, he was always ready to help any old person or child. But he did like playing jokes and making fun. Once, I remember, he dressed himself as a lady visitor to the town and asked to see "the rector who gave such wonderful sermons". My father believed him, I mean her, and offered her all his sermons about Napoleon. Then he made Peter copy them all out for her instead of going fishing! How I wanted to laugh!'

'Did Miss Jenkyns know about these jokes?' I asked.

'Oh, no! I was the only one who knew. Peter used to say that the old ladies in the town needed something to talk about. But sometimes he didn't tell me, and at last a terrible, sad thing happened . . .'

Miss Matty went to the door and opened it. There was no one there. She rang the bell, and told Martha to go across the town for some eggs. 'I'll lock the door when you've gone,

Martha. You're not afraid to go, are you?'

'Oh no, madam! Jem Hearn will be proud to come with me.'

Miss Matty's eyes widened. She was still a little worried by the idea of Martha having a follower.

'I'll put out the candle, my dear,' she said to me as soon as we were alone. 'We can talk just as well by firelight.

'Well, it was a quiet spring day, I remember. Deborah had gone away for a fortnight, and my father was visiting some sick people in the town. Peter, it seems, went up to Deborah's room and dressed himself in her old dress and shawl and bonnet. And he made the pillow from her bed into – are you sure we locked the door, my dear? – into a little baby with long, white clothes. And he walked up and down outside, and nursed the pillow just like a baby, and talked to it in the way people do to babies. Then, oh my dear, my father came back and saw a crowd of people looking into our garden. At first, he thought they were looking at his flowers. Then he saw Peter. His face went white, he was so angry. He tore the clothes off Peter's back and threw the pillow into the crowd and, in front of everyone, he beat Peter with his walking-stick. My dear, that boy's joke, on that spring day, broke my mother's heart and changed my father for ever.

'Peter stood still until my father had finished. Then he walked slowly into the house, put his arms round my mother and kissed her. Before she could speak, he had gone. We couldn't understand it.

'She sent me to ask my father what had happened. "Tell

27

My father saw a crowd of people looking into our garden.

your mother I have beaten Peter," he said.

'When I told her, my pretty little mother sat down, very white. Then we began to search the house. It was a big old house, and we searched and searched. "Peter, dear!" my mother called softly. "It's only me." Then her cry grew louder. "Peter! Peter! Where are you?"

'The afternoon went on. The servants joined the search. My father sat with his head in his hands. When it was nearly dark, he got up. "Molly," he began, "I did not mean all this to happen—" As he looked at my mother's poor white face,

tears came into his eyes. And then she took my father's great
hand in her little one and led him along, from room to room,
through the house and garden, everywhere. I sent someone
to Mr Holbrook to ask if Peter was at his house. Mr Holbrook
was Miss Pole's cousin, you know, and he had been very
kind to Peter and had taught him how to fish. But Peter
wasn't there or anywhere in Cranford.'

'Where was he?' I asked.

'He had gone to Liverpool. There was war then, and some
of the king's ships were at the mouth of the River Mersey.

They were glad to have a fine, tall boy like Peter. The captain wrote to my father, and Peter wrote to my mother. Those letters are here somewhere too.'

We lit the candle and found them. The captain's letter told the parents to come to Liverpool immediately if they wished to see their boy. And Peter's letter begged his mother to come. '*Mother! We may go into battle. I hope we shall, and that we'll defeat those French. I must see you first, though.*'

'But my father and mother arrived too late,' said Miss Matty. 'The ship had gone.'

We sat silently for a while. Peter's ship went to the Mediterranean, Miss Matty told me at last, and later he was sent to India. Her mother had never been strong and she died less than a year after he went away.

'And the day after her death – yes, the day after – a packet arrived for her from India from her poor boy. It was a large, soft, white shawl. Deborah took it in to my father and he held it in his hands and said, "She always wanted a shawl like this. We'll bury her in it. Peter would like that."

'On the day of my mother's funeral, Deborah told me that she would never marry and leave my father, even if she had a hundred offers of marriage. This wasn't very likely, of course – I don't think she had one; but it was good of her to say it. She was a wonderful daughter. She did everything for my father.'

'Did Mr Peter ever come home?'

'Yes, once. My father took him into every house in

Cranford, he was so proud of him in his uniform. Deborah used to smile (I don't think we ever laughed again after my mother's death) and say she was not needed any more.'

'And then?' I asked.

'Then Peter went to sea again. And after a while my father died, and we had to come to this small house with just one servant instead of four. Poor Deborah!'

'And Mr Peter?'

'Oh, there was some great war in India and we've never heard of him since then. I believe he's dead, though sometimes when all the house is quiet, I think I hear him coming up the street. But the sound always goes past and Peter never comes . . . Is that Martha? I'll go, my dear. No, I don't need a candle . . .'

'Was it Martha?' I asked when she returned.

'Yes. And I heard such a strange noise when I opened the door.'

'Where?'

'In the street, just outside. It sounded like— '

'Talking?'

'No! Kissing!'

5

'Your ladyship'

One morning, before twelve o'clock, Martha came up and said that Miss Betty Barker would like to speak to her mistress. Miss Matty disappeared to change her cap and Miss Barker came upstairs, apologizing again and again for her visit.

Miss Betty Barker was the daughter of the late Mr Jenkyns's clerk. She and her elder sister (who had worked for Mrs Jamieson) had been ladies' maids. Later, they had had a hat-shop, with Lady Arley as a customer. When the sister died, Miss Betty shut the shop and became the most wonderfully dressed lady in Cranford – wearing all the bonnets and caps and ribbons that were left on her shelves.

And now Miss Betty Barker had called to invite Miss Matty to tea on the following Tuesday. She had already invited the Honourable Mrs Jamieson, she said. She invited me too – though she was clearly worried that, as my father had gone to live in Drumble, he was now in 'that awful cotton trade'. Miss Barker's own days in 'trade' had finished several years ago, and she now liked to think of herself as one of the ladies of Cranford – though she was always very respectful towards the 'best' families.

'Mrs Jamieson is coming?' asked Miss Matty.

'Yes. It's most kind of ladies such as Mrs Jamieson and yourself to call on someone like myself . . .' Miss Barker began to apologize again.

She was now going, she told Miss Matty, to see Mrs Forrester and Miss Pole. 'Of course, I invited you first, madam, as a rector's daughter. But we must not forget that Mrs Forrester is related to the Bigges of Bigelow Hall. So I shall invite her before I invite Miss Pole.'

'And Mrs Fitz-Adam?' asked Miss Matty.

'No, madam. I have great respect for Mrs Fitz-Adam but Mrs Jamieson would not like to meet her, I think.' Miss Barker rose. 'Will you come to my little house at half-past six, Miss Matilda? That's when Mrs Jamieson has promised to come.' Miss Betty Barker curtsied and left.

Mrs Fitz-Adam was the sister of Mr Hoggins, the Cranford doctor. Their parents were respectable farmers, but they did not belong to Cranford 'society'. When Miss Mary Hoggins married Mr Fitz-Adam (whoever he was), she left the town. Then, after his death, she reappeared as a widow in black silk, and rented a large old house.

I remember that the ladies of Cranford met to discuss whether they should visit her. The matter had still not been decided when Miss Jenkyns died.

'However, as most of us are either unmarried or widows without children,' Miss Pole had said, 'we'll soon have no society at all if we don't change our rules a little.'

So everybody called on Mrs Fitz-Adam – everybody except Mrs Jamieson, who was related, of course, to the family of a

33

lord. She used to show how important she was by never seeing or speaking to Mrs Fitz-Adam when they met at the Cranford parties. Mrs Fitz-Adam was large and, when Mrs Jamieson came in, she always stood up and curtsied very low. But Mrs Jamieson still did not see her.

It was a bright spring evening when the four of us – Miss Matty, Mrs Forrester, Miss Pole and myself – met outside Miss Barker's house. We heard loud whispers inside. 'Wait, Peggy! Wait until I've run upstairs! Then, when I cough, open the door.'

The cough came. Immediately, a maid opened the door and showed us into a small room that had been the shop. We uncovered our caps and shook our skirts. Then we walked up the narrow stairs to Miss Barker's drawing-room. Kind, gentle Mrs Forrester was given the second place of honour. The first place, of course, was for the Honourable Mrs Jamieson, who soon came heavily up the stairs.

And now Miss Betty Barker was a proud, happy woman! Peggy the maid came in with a generous trayful of cake. Did the ladies think this vulgar, I wondered? Clearly, they did not. All the cake disappeared. I saw Mrs Jamieson eat three pieces, slowly, with an expression not unlike a cow's.

After tea, the ladies played cards – all except myself (I was rather afraid of the Cranford ladies at cards) and Mrs Jamieson, who fell asleep in her armchair. I enjoyed watching the four ladies' caps at the card-table, and hearing Miss Barker's 'Sssh, ladies, please! Mrs Jamieson is asleep!'

Mrs Jamieson still did not see her.

Then the door opened. Mrs Jamieson woke up, and Peggy came in with another trayful of good things! We did not usually eat supper, but politely (and hungrily) we gave in. We even accepted a little drink . . .

Suddenly, Mrs Jamieson gave us some news. 'My sister-in-law, Lady Glenmire, is coming to stay with me.'

'Indeed!' said everyone. Then there was a pause. Did we have the right dresses in which to appear before Lady Glenmire? We felt very excited and unsure.

Not long after this, the little party came to an end. Mrs Jamieson got into her carriage, and the rest of us walked home along the quiet little street.

At twelve next day, Miss Pole appeared at Miss Matty's. 'What should we call Lady Glenmire?' she asked anxiously. 'Must we say "your ladyship" instead of just "you"? And "my lady" instead of "madam"? You knew Lady Arley, Miss Matty. What did you call her?'

Poor Miss Matty! She took off her glasses and she put them on again, but she could not remember. 'It was so long ago,' she said, 'and I only ever saw her twice. Oh dear, how stupid I am!'

'Then I'd better go and ask Mrs Forrester,' said Miss Pole. 'We don't want Lady Glenmire to think we know nothing about polite society here in Cranford.'

'Who is Lady Glenmire exactly?' I asked when Miss Pole had gone.

'My dear, she's the widow of Lord Glenmire, and *he* was Mr Jamieson's elder brother. But I wonder what we should call her . . .'

Miss Matty's worrying was unnecessary. Mrs Jamieson was the next person who arrived – and Mrs Jamieson, most impolitely, made it clear that she did not wish the Cranford ladies to visit her sister-in-law.

'Well!' said Miss Pole, who returned soon afterwards, very red and annoyed. 'So we must not call on Lady Glenmire! Only the best county families are acceptable visitors, and Cranford society is not good enough, it seems! Yes, I met Mrs Jamieson on her way from here to Mrs Forrester's, and she told me. I wish I'd said something sharp. Who is this Lady Glenmire anyway? Only the widow of a Scottish lord, and the fifth daughter of some Mr Campbell.' Miss Pole, usually so kind and calm, was really annoyed. 'And I ordered a new cap this morning, in order to be quite ready!'

When we came out of church on Lady Glenmire's first Sunday in Cranford, we carefully turned our backs on Mrs Jamieson and her sister-in-law. We did not even look at Lady Glenmire, though we very much wanted to know what she was like.

Afterwards we questioned Martha, however, and Martha had used her eyes well. 'The little lady with Mrs Jamieson, you mean? She was wearing a rather old black silk dress and she had bright black eyes. She looked up and down the church, like a bird, and lifted her skirts when she came out, very quick and sharp. She's more like the landlady at the George Inn than a real lady!'

'Sssh, Martha!' said Miss Matty. 'That's not respectful.'

Another Sunday passed, and we still turned away from the two widows. By this time, Lady Glenmire was perhaps getting a little bored at Mrs Jamieson's. Whatever the reason, Mrs Jamieson suddenly sent us invitations to a small party. Her man Mulliner brought them himself, coming as usual to

*We carefully turned our backs
on Mrs Jamieson and her sister-in-law.*

the front door instead of to the back like other servants.

Miss Matty and I quietly decided not to accept ours. But before we had replied, Miss Pole arrived.

'The invitation is for Tuesday,' Miss Matty told her. 'If you bring your knitting and drink tea with us that evening, I'll have a good reason to refuse.'

I saw Miss Pole's expression change. 'You're not going? Oh, Miss Matty, you must go! We can't let Mrs Jamieson think we care about anything she says. I'm ready to "forgive and forget". As a rector's daughter, you should do the same . . .'

The fact was that Miss Pole had a new cap and wanted to wear it. So in the end Miss Matty bought a new cap too, and so did Mrs Forrester, and we all went to Mrs Jamieson's party.

Mrs Jamieson's drawing-room was not a comfortable room. Neither she nor Mulliner – of whom she seemed a little afraid – did anything to make us feel welcome. Lady Glenmire arranged the chairs agreeably for us, however. Now that we could look at her, we saw that she was a bright little woman of middle age, who had been very pretty when she was young.

We were all silent at first, unsure what to say to 'my lady'. At last Miss Pole spoke. 'Has your ladyship seen the dear Queen lately?' she asked, and looked proudly round at us.

'I've never seen her in my life,' said Lady Glenmire in a sweet Scottish voice. 'In fact, I've only been to London twice. Have you been to Edinburgh?' she asked hopefully.

None of us had, but Miss Pole had an uncle who once passed a night there. So that was very pleasant.

Mrs Jamieson meanwhile began to wonder aloud why Mulliner did not bring in the tea, but she did not want to trouble Mulliner by ringing the bell. In the end, Lady Glenmire grew quite impatient, and rang the bell herself. Mulliner appeared, looking surprised.

'Lady Glenmire rang,' said Mrs Jamieson. 'I believe it was for tea.'

Tea came at last. The plates were very thin and fine. So was the bread-and-butter. We were grateful to Lady Glenmire for ordering more of it, and a comfortable conversation developed. Soon the ladies were playing cards happily together and even Miss Pole quite forgot to say 'my lady' and 'your ladyship'.

We learnt during the evening that Lady Glenmire had no plans to return quickly to Edinburgh. We were rather glad. We liked her.

'Isn't walking very unpleasant?' asked Mrs Jamieson as we prepared to leave. (This was a regular question from her as she had a carriage and never walked anywhere.)

'Oh no, not at night!' said Miss Pole. 'Such peace after the excitement of a party!' said Mrs Forrester. 'The stars are so beautiful!' said Miss Matty.

So we walked home under the stars, feeling very grand, after drinking tea with 'my lady'.

'My dears,' said Miss Pole next day, very pleased. 'Did you notice her dress? So inexpensive!'

6

Signor Brunoni

Soon after Mrs Jamieson's party, my father became ill and I had to go home to Drumble. I stayed there for most of the rest of the year. Then, at the end of November, I received a mysterious letter from Miss Matty.

She hoped my father was well, she wrote, and could I tell her if turbans were fashionable? Something so exciting was going to happen. She must have a new cap, and perhaps she was too old to care about such things, but she would very much like a turban . . . Oh, and would I like to come for a visit next Tuesday? Sea-green was her favourite colour . . .

Fortunately, there was a note of explanation at the end: *'My dear, Signor Brunoni is going to show his wonderful magic at Cranford Assembly Room next Wednesday evening.'*

I was very glad to accept the invitation from my dear Miss Matty, and very anxious to stop her wearing a great turban on her gentle little head. So I bought her a pretty blue cap instead, which disappointed her terribly. She followed me into my bedroom, and I think she was still hoping to find a sea-green turban somewhere inside my cap-box.

'I'm sure you tried, my dear,' she said sadly, looking at the cap. 'It's just like the caps all the ladies in Cranford are wearing. I suppose turbans haven't arrived in Drumble yet?'

41

She left the room to welcome Miss Pole and Mrs Forrester to tea. 'It was silly to expect anything fashionable from the Drumble shops, I suppose,' I heard her tell them. 'Poor girl! She did her best.'

But Miss Pole had had an adventure, and was waiting impatiently to describe it. 'I happened to go into the George Inn today,' she began when I entered. 'My Betty has a cousin who's a maid there, you know, and I thought Betty would like news of her. Well, there was no one around, so I walked up the stairs and into the Assembly Room. And there I saw that people were getting things ready for tomorrow night. I was just going behind the curtain, by mistake, when a gentleman stepped forward. He asked in very pretty broken English if he could help me. He didn't want me to see behind that curtain, it seemed. So, most politely, he showed me out of the room.

'Wait! You've not heard all my story yet! As I was going downstairs again, I met Betty's cousin – and she told me that the gentleman was Signor Brunoni! And then, it was so strange, I met the same gentleman again on his way *up*!'

So Miss Pole had met the conjurer himself! Oh, what questions we asked her! 'Did he have a beard?' 'Was he young or old?' 'Was he fair or dark?' 'What did he really look like?'

We talked about magic all evening. Miss Pole did not believe in it: conjurers' tricks could be learnt from a book, she said. Mrs Forrester believed in magic, ghosts, everything. Miss Matty was not sure what she believed – and always agreed with the last speaker.

The next evening, the four of us met in gentle excitement at the entrance to the George Inn. From there, we went upstairs together to the Assembly Room. Miss Pole asked a waiter if any of the county families were coming, as they would expect to sit in the front row. When he shook his head, Miss Matty and Mrs Forrester sat in the front row, where Lady Glenmire and Mrs Jamieson soon joined them. Miss Pole and I sat immediately behind, in the second row. All the shopkeepers sat together at the back, talking and laughing happily. I got rather bored with waiting, and wanted to turn round and look at them, but Miss Pole begged me not to. It was not the correct way to behave, she said. So our group was dull and quiet. Mrs Jamieson fell asleep.

Finally, the curtain went up. We saw, at a little table, a fantastic-looking gentleman in Turkish dress, with a long beard and a turban.

Miss Matty looked at me. 'You see, my dear, people *are* wearing turbans,' she said sadly.

But we had no time for more conversation. The Grand Turk rose and said he was Signor Brunoni.

'I don't believe him!' said Miss Pole loudly. 'Signor Brunoni didn't have a beard.'

This woke Mrs Jamieson. She opened her eyes wide, and the Grand Turk, who had looked crossly at Miss Pole, began his magic.

Now we were surprised and delighted – all except Miss Pole. Such tricks! I could not imagine, even with Miss Pole's

We were surprised and delighted – all except Miss Pole.

whispered explanations, how he did them. It was all so wonderful that Miss Matty and Mrs Forrester became anxious.

'Do you think it's quite right for us to come and see such things?' I heard Miss Matty whisper. 'Is there something not quite—?' She shook her head.

'I was asking myself the same question,' Mrs Forrester whispered back. 'It's so very strange. I'm certain that was one of my ribbons on his table just now . . .'

Suddenly, Miss Matty half-turned towards me. 'My dear, will you look round (you don't live in the town – no one will talk about it), and see if Mr Hayter the rector is here?'

I looked round and saw the tall, thin rector among his schoolboys. His kind face was all smiles, and the boys were laughing. I told Miss Matty that the Church approved of Signor Brunoni, and she began to enjoy herself again.

⊰⊱

Soon the excitement was over. Signor Brunoni disappeared from Cranford, and the only result of his visit was a new readiness among the ladies to believe in strange happenings.

Six weeks later, however, Miss Pole had another adventure. Lady Glenmire was now a friend, and one morning the two of them went out walking together. About three miles from Cranford, on the road to London, they stopped at a small inn called the 'Rising Sun' to ask the way across the fields.

'A little girl came in while we were there,' Miss Pole told us that afternoon. 'The landlady said she was the only child of a married couple who were staying in the house. Now, listen to this! About six weeks ago, the landlady said, a horse-and-cart turned over right outside the inn. In the cart were two men, one woman and this child, plus a great box of strange things. One of the men, the child's father, was hurt and has been at the inn ever since. The other man (his twin brother, she believes) drove quickly away in the cart, and took the box with him. Well, my dears, the man who was hurt is Signor Brunoni! We met his wife – a good, honest person – and she says his real name is Samuel Brown!'

The conjurer's family, it seemed, now had no money, and Miss Pole and Lady Glenmire had decided to help them. In fact, Lady Glenmire had gone straight to Mr Hoggins, the Cranford doctor, to beg him to ride over to the 'Rising Sun' that same afternoon.

Miss Matty and I were now as interested in this news as Miss Pole was. So was Mrs Forrester when she heard about it. The ladies waited anxiously for Mr Hoggins's opinion. When Mr Hoggins said that, with care, the conjurer would get better, they brought him to Cranford. Lady Glenmire promised to pay the doctor's bills. Miss Pole found comfortable lodgings for the family. Miss Matty sent a carriage for them. Mrs Forrester was not too proud to help, either. Though she was related to the Bigges of Bigelow Hall, here she was, taking nice things to eat to a poor, sick conjurer! It was wonderful to see all the kindness.

Soon Miss Matty was making a coloured ball for the little girl, Phoebe, to play with. 'I've always been so fond of children,' she said to me sadly as we sat by the fire, 'and I dream sometimes that I have a little child of my own . . . I didn't expect to be "Miss Matty Jenkyns" all my life, you know,' she went on after a pause. 'But the person I expected to marry is dead, and he never knew why I refused him. Ah well, it doesn't matter now. I am very happy, my dear. I have such kind friends,' she continued, taking my hand.

As I knew about Mr Holbrook, I could think of nothing suitable to say, and we were both silent.

One day soon after this, I asked the conjurer's wife if Miss Pole's story about twin brothers was true.

'Quite true,' she said, 'though I don't know how anyone can mistake Thomas for the real Signor Brunoni. Thomas is a good man, and he paid all our bills at the Rising Sun, but he can't do the ball-trick as well as my husband can. And he's never been in India, so he doesn't know how to wear a turban.'

'Have you been in India?' said I, rather surprised.

She told me that her husband had been sent there in the army. She had gone with him but, one after another, their children had died out there. 'That cruel India!' she said. 'I was going mad. When Phoebe, this last child, was born, I told my Sam I must return to England.'

So, carrying her baby, she had left her husband to go to Calcutta. She had walked a hundred miles, from village to village. People had given her food and milk, she said. And once, when the baby was ill, she had been helped by a kind Englishman living among the Indians.

'And you reached Calcutta safely?'

'Yes. And after two years, Sam was able to come home. He'd learnt some tricks from an Indian, so he began to work as a conjurer. Then, after a while, he employed his twin brother to help him.'

'And Phoebe was well again?'

'Yes. That good kind Aga Jenkyns at Chunderabaddad had helped me to save her.'

'Jenkyns!' said I.

'Yes. Jenkyns. I'm beginning to think all people with that name are kind. Here in Cranford, there's that nice old lady who comes every day to see Phoebe!'

7

Sudden news

An idea had come into my head. Was Peter Jenkyns of Cranford now the Aga Jenkyns of Chunderabaddad? Could it be possible? I decided to ask the Cranford ladies some questions, without explaining what I suspected.

I did not learn much. Miss Pole believed that Peter had become something important in Tibet. Mrs Forrester said he had been rather handsome. They both thought the last news of him had come from India. That was almost all I discovered.

Meanwhile, however, something extraordinary was going on around us and we all, even Miss Pole, failed to notice! I remember the morning she came to tell us. It was nearly calling-time. Miss Matty and I had just been discussing Signor Brunoni and that clever Mr Hoggins when someone knocked at the door.

We were hurrying to change our caps when Miss Pole ran up the stairs. 'It's not twelve, I know,' she called, 'but I *must* speak to you. What *do* you think? Mr Hoggins is going to marry Lady Glenmire!'

'Marry?!' we said.

'Marry! I heard it in Mr Johnson's shop.'

'Perhaps it's not true,' said Miss Matty hopefully.

'It's true,' said Miss Pole. 'I went straight to Mrs Fitz-Adam, and she said her brother and Lady Glenmire had come to an understanding. "Understanding"! Such a vulgar word! But my lady will have to hear many vulgar words now. I believe Mr Hoggins drinks beer at supper every night . . .'

'Marry!' repeated Miss Matty. 'Well! Two people that we know going to be married. It's coming very near!'

'I'm not surprised that Mr Hoggins likes her,' I said. 'But how can *she* like Mr Hoggins?'

'Oh, Mr Hoggins is rich and very pleasant-looking,' said Miss Matty, 'and very kind.'

We began to wonder what the Honourable Mrs Jamieson would say. Mrs Jamieson had recently gone down to Cheltenham in the care of Mulliner, leaving Lady Glenmire to manage her house and to stop her maids taking followers. And while she was away, Lady Glenmire had herself taken a

'Mr Hoggins is going to marry Lady Glenmire!' called Miss Pole.

follower! A follower whom Mrs Jamieson thought was vulgar and not good enough for Cranford society! Had Mr Hoggins ever visited Lady Glenmire at Mrs Jamieson's house, we wondered? Or had they only met at the lodgings of the poor sick conjurer? Certainly, they had both been very kind to him.

Well! What next? When would the wedding be? How could servants announce a married couple as 'Lady Glenmire and Mr Hoggins'? Would anyone visit the couple? Oh dear, would we have to choose between visiting dull Mrs Jamieson and bright Lady Glenmire?

Next time we saw Lady Glenmire, in church, she looked happy and younger than before. Mr Hoggins too looked happy, and he was wearing his first new pair of boots for twenty-five years. But none of the Cranford ladies said anything to either of them about their marriage. Until Mrs Jamieson returned, indeed, we did not know what to say.

But it was now March, and Mr Johnson announced the arrival of the spring fashions at his shop. Miss Matty had been waiting for this before buying herself a new silk dress. In our excitement we forgot, for the moment, about Lady Glenmire.

On the Tuesday on which Mr Johnson was going to show the new fashions, two letters were waiting for us on the breakfast table. One was to me from my father – a dull, businessman's letter. There were unpleasant reports about the Town and County Bank, he wrote, and he hoped Miss Matty did not still have shares in it. He had warned her sister years ago not to put money into that bank, but she had not listened to his advice.

'Who is your letter from, my dear?' asked Miss Matty. 'Mine is from the Town and County Bank, asking me to an

51

important meeting of the shareholders in Drumble on Thursday. It's kind of them to remember me.'

I was alarmed at this 'important meeting', and was afraid that my father's fears were right. However, bad news always came fast enough, so I decided to say nothing for the moment. I simply told Miss Matty that my father sent his best wishes, then I changed the conversation. 'What time should we go to see the fashions?' I asked.

'Well, the correct time to go is after twelve o'clock,' she said. 'But then all Cranford will be there, and I'd rather not look at dresses and caps in front of everyone. So let's go this morning after breakfast. I need half a pound of tea. We can buy that, and choose the silk for my new dress. Then we can go quietly upstairs, look at the fashions and decide the style for my dress.'

The young men at Mr Johnson's wore their best clothes and their best smiles. Miss Matty bought her tea, then began looking at the silks. It was Cranford's market-day, and many country people came into the shop.

One honest-looking man stood next to us and asked to look at some shawls for his wife. He hesitated. Miss Matty hesitated too. She would like a sea-green silk. No, that lovely red. No, that bright yellow . . .

Our neighbour finally chose a shawl and held out a five-pound note.

The shop-boy looked at the note. 'Town and County Bank! I think we were warned this morning not to accept this bank's notes. I'll just ask Mr Johnson . . .'

'What!' The poor farmer could not believe it.

Miss Matty forgot her new silk dress. 'Which bank did your note belong to?' she asked him.

'Town and County.'

'Mr Johnson's very sorry, Mr Dobson,' the boy said as he brought the note back, 'but the bank's notes are worthless.'

'I don't understand,' Miss Matty said to me in a low voice. 'Town and County is my bank, isn't it?'

'Yes . . . This yellow silk will match the ribbons in your new cap,' I continued quickly, holding it up and wishing the man would go away.

'Never mind the silks for a moment, dear,' she said, putting her hand gently on mine and looking at the farmer. 'I'll give you five pound coins for your note, Mr Dobson,' she said. 'But there must be some mistake. I'm a shareholder in that bank and I've not been told about any problem.'

The shop-boy whispered across the table to Miss Matty. She looked at him uncertainly. 'I don't understand business,' she said. 'But if honest people are going to lose their money because they have our notes, then . . . Oh, I can't explain myself. Just give me your note, please, Mr Dobson, and then you can take the shawl for your wife.'

The farmer looked at her gratefully, but hesitated for a moment. 'I wouldn't like somebody else to lose money instead of me,' he said. 'But, you see, madam, five pounds is a lot of money to a man with a family.'

'I'm sure there is a mistake,' said Miss Matty quietly, 'and in a few days everything will be all right.' She pushed her five gold coins towards the farmer, who slowly put down his note. 'Thank you,' Miss Matty said. 'I'll wait a day or two before I buy any of these silks,' she told the boy. 'My dear, will you come upstairs and see the fashions?'

Miss Matty looked with great interest at all the new dresses

'*Just give me your note, please, Mr Dobson,*' said Miss Matty.

and bonnets and shawls. She seemed unworried by what had happened downstairs. But as we came down through the shop, Mr Johnson was waiting for us. It was true, he said, the bank was in serious trouble. Miss Matty showed no surprise or alarm. Cranford ladies thought it was vulgar to show their feelings in a shop.

However, we walked home very silently and neither of us ate much dinner. Later, in the drawing-room, Miss Matty unlocked her desk and began to look through her bills and papers. After a while, she came and sat next to me, by the fire. I put my hand into hers. She held it, but did not speak.

At last she said, 'If that bank goes wrong, I'll lose £149 a year. I'll only have £13 a year left.' It was too dark to see her face, but I knew that she was crying. 'Oh, I'm so glad poor Deborah is not here!' That was all she said about the sister who had put their money in that unlucky bank.

We lit the candle later than usual that day. After tea, however, we talked about Lady Glenmire. Miss Matty had begun to think it was a good idea for her to marry Mr Hoggins. 'A man knows what to do when there are problems,' she said. 'And Mr Hoggins, though a little rough, is very nice. I've known good, clever people who were not "in society" but were both true and loving . . .'

She began to day-dream about Mr Holbrook, and I did not stop her. I had decided what to do. That night after she went to bed, I lit the candle again and sat down in the drawing-room to write a letter to the Aga Jenkyns. The church clock struck two before I had finished.

The next morning news came that the Town and County Bank had failed. Miss Matty had lost all her money. She now had only about one pound a month on which to live. 'But many poor people have less,' she said. 'Poor Martha! I think she'll be sorry to leave me.' She smiled at me through her tears, and I think she wanted me to see only the smile, not the tears.

8
True friends

While Miss Matty went downstairs to tell Martha, I quietly picked up my letter and went to Signor Brunoni's lodgings. The signor was now well enough to leave Cranford and, before he disappeared, I needed an exact address for the Aga Jenkyns in Chunderabaddad.

I then posted my letter to India, and hurried back home. Martha, in tears now herself, pulled me into the kitchen.

'I'll never leave her! I won't. "You may not know when you've got a good servant," I told her, "but I know when I've got a good mistress!" I've money in the Savings Bank, and I'm not going to leave Miss Matty.'

What should I say? Miss Matty needed this kind woman. 'But, Martha, I don't think Miss Matty will even have enough money to buy your food.'

'Not enough for food?!' Martha sat down on the nearest chair and cried aloud.

Upstairs, Miss Matty was very quiet and sad. We decided to ask my father to come and advise her. So I wrote another letter, and then we tried to make plans.

Miss Matty just wanted to sell most of her things, rent a single room somewhere and live quietly on the money that remained.

I wanted something better for her. She needed money and I wondered how she, a lady, could earn some. By teaching? She loved children, but she could not sing or draw or sew. Perhaps she could teach reading? No. When she read aloud, she had to cough before each long word. Writing? Her spelling was terrible! No. There was nothing she could teach the children of Cranford, I decided, except quiet goodness.

Dinner was announced by Martha, still crying. Dear, rough Martha! She now spoke to 58-year-old Miss Matty as kindly as to a child, and she had gone out and bought eggs and butter with her own money to cook her something special.

We did not talk much that afternoon, but when Martha brought our tea, I had an idea. Miss Matty could sell tea! Tea was not dirty, or heavy. And no shop-window would be necessary, only a small sign. The one thing against my plan was the buying and selling involved. Miss Matty would be in trade. Would she ever agree to that?

Suddenly, we heard a noise on the stairs and some whispering. Then Martha came in, pulling a great tall young man who was red with shyness.

'Please, madam, he's only Jem Hearn,' said Martha, breathing hard. 'And please, madam, he wants to marry me immediately. And we want to rent a house and have just one quiet lodger, to help us with the money. And, dear Miss Matty, will you be that lodger and stay with us? Jem wants it as much as I do.' She turned to him. 'You stupid great thing! Why don't you speak? . . . He wants the same as I do, but he's shy in front of ladies,' she explained.

'It's not that,' said Jem. 'It's just that, well, I didn't expect to marry so soon. Martha moves so fast when she has an idea in her head . . .'

Martha pushed him with her elbow. 'Please, madam, don't listen to him. He asked me only last night to marry him, but I said I couldn't yet, so now he's just surprised at the suddenness of it. But you know, Jem, you want a lodger as much as I do.' Another great push.

'Yes!' he said. 'And I don't mind marrying Martha, madam.'

'You've never stopped asking me,' cried Martha, 'and now you're making me look silly in front of my mistress!'

'Now, now, Martha,' said Jem, trying to hold her hand. 'It's just that a man needs time!' He turned to Miss Matty. 'I always expected Martha to be my wife – one day,' he said. 'I've great respect for everyone who's been kind to her, madam, and she's often said you're the kindest lady in the world. If you'd lodge with us, we'd try to make you comfortable . . .'

Miss Matty had been very busy with taking off her glasses,

wiping them, and putting them on again. All she could say was, 'You mustn't hurry into marriage just because of me. Marriage is a very serious thing . . .'

'But Miss Matty will think about your plan,' I said quickly, 'and she can never forget your kindness.'

'I don't mind marrying Martha,' Jem said.

'I'm very willing, madam, though I don't explain myself well,' Jem replied. 'So, Martha, my girl,' he whispered, 'why do you go on crying and pushing me?'

Martha, annoyed, ran out of the room and was followed by her lover. Miss Matty then sat down and cried. The idea of Martha marrying so soon was such a surprise, she said. She would never forgive herself if the poor girl hurried into marriage because of her. I think I was more sorry for Jem of the two . . .

The next morning, very early, I received a mysterious note from Miss Pole, commanding me to come secretly to her house at eleven o'clock.

I went. The door was opened by Miss Pole's little maid in her Sunday clothes. Upstairs in the drawing-room, the table was covered with the best green card-cloth, and there were writing materials on it. Miss Pole was dressed for visitors. Mrs Forrester was already there, and then Mrs Fitz-Adam appeared, red with walking and excitement.

Miss Pole coughed. She arranged all of us at the table, with me opposite her. Then she asked me if it was true that Miss Matty had lost all her money.

'Yes, it's true,' I said, and I never saw sadder faces than the three around me.

'I wish Mrs Jamieson was here!' said Mrs Forrester.

Mrs Fitz-Adam clearly did not agree, and Miss Pole was not pleased. 'Even without Mrs Jamieson,' she said, 'we, the ladies of Cranford, can do something.'

She turned to me. 'Miss Smith,' she continued (I was

usually known as Mary), 'I talked privately yesterday afternoon to these ladies about what has happened to our friend. None of us is vulgarly rich, but we shall all be pleased – truly pleased, Mary! – to give what we can to help Miss Matilda Jenkyns.' Here Miss Pole had to wipe her glasses.

'We wish, however, to give our little bits of money secretly, in order not to hurt any feelings. This is why we asked you to meet us. Your father, we believe, is Miss Jenkyns's adviser. We would like him to arrange for her to receive the money without knowing that it comes from us.' Miss Pole looked round at the little assembly. 'And now, ladies, while Miss Smith considers how to reply, allow me to offer you some bread-and-butter.'

I did not reply very grandly. I just said that I would tell my father, and began to cry. The ladies cried too. Even Miss Pole.

Mrs Forrester was the first to speak again. 'I'll write down what money I can give. I wish it was more, my dear Mary. Indeed I do!'

Now I saw why paper and pens had been put on the table. Every lady privately wrote down what she could give each year, signed her paper and passed it to me. If the plan was accepted, my father would open the papers. If not, he would return them to their writers.

I got up to leave, but each lady wanted to speak to me by herself. Miss Pole kept me in the drawing-room, to say she had heard that Mrs Jamieson was coming home – very displeased with her sister-in-law, who was returning to

61

Edinburgh that same afternoon. Of course, she could not say this in front of Mrs Fitz-Adam, who, as Mr Hoggins's sister, would not like to hear of anybody being angry about her brother's marriage.

Downstairs, Mrs Forrester was waiting. The poor old lady was trembling. She herself had less than £100 a year, she whispered, so she had only been able to promise Miss Matty £5 on her paper. She wished she was rich. She wished she could help dear Miss Matty more . . .

And then Mrs Fitz-Adam stopped me outside the house – to say almost the opposite. She had not liked to write down all she could afford and was ready to give.

'Miss Matty was such a fine young lady,' she explained, 'when I was just a country girl coming to Cranford market. One day, I remember, I met her just outside the town. She was walking, and a gentleman rode beside her and was talking to her. She was looking down at some flowers she had picked, and I think she was crying. But she turned and ran after me to ask – oh, so kindly – about my poor mother, who was dying. Miss Matty was the rector's daughter, and it was such an honour that she spoke to me in that pretty way.

'So do please think how I can give her a little more without anyone knowing, my dear. And my brother will be her doctor for nothing. He and her ladyship are ready to do anything for her. We all are.'

I was so anxious to get home to Miss Matty that I made all kinds of promises. But Miss Matty had not missed me. She was busy preparing to leave her house, and I think she was pleased to be doing something. Whenever she thought about Mr Dobson with his five-pound note, she said, she felt so dishonest! She was sure the bankers themselves must feel terrible . . .

My father arrived next morning, and when we were alone, I told him about Martha's plan and my meeting with the Cranford ladies.

My father brushed his hand across his eyes. 'See, Mary,' he said, 'how a good life makes friends all round. I could write a sermon about it if I was the rector!'

He and I decided that, if everyone agreed, Martha and Jem would marry as soon as possible and rent Miss Matty's house with the money given by the Cranford ladies. Then Martha could use whatever Miss Matty paid for her lodgings to make her comfortable.

I told my father my idea that Miss Matty could sell tea, and he liked it. One of the rooms downstairs could become a shop, he said enthusiastically. It could have a glass door and Miss Matty could sit behind a table . . .

Miss Matty patiently accepted all we arranged. She even agreed to sell tea. 'Though I doubt that I'll do it very well,' she said. 'I'd so much rather sell sweets to children!'

9

A happy return

Mrs Jamieson, when she returned, considered Miss Matty's situation for two or three days. Then she kindly gave her approval and allowed Miss Matty to sell tea and still remain in Cranford society, although she would be in trade. I think she was trying to annoy Lady Glenmire, by showing that a married woman comes down to her husband's level in society. An unmarried woman like Miss Matty, however, could keep the level that her father had. So Cranford was allowed to visit Miss Matty; and, whether allowed or not, it was going to visit Lady Glenmire.

But then we learnt that 'Mr and Mrs Hoggins' were going to return the following week. 'Mrs Hoggins', not 'Lady Glenmire'! Mrs Jamieson was pleased. 'That woman' never had any taste, she said. But 'that woman' and her new husband looked very happy on Sunday at church – and we did not turn our faces away from them as Mrs Jamieson did.

Miss Matty sold a lot of her furniture, though 'an unknown friend' (Mrs Fitz-Adam, I suspected) bought some favourite pieces back for her. The rector, too, bought the late Mr Jenkyns's library and then offered some of the books back to Miss Matty, saying he had not enough shelves for them all.

The downstairs room was changed into a shop, as agreed,

Everyone suddenly seemed to need tea.

and we put a very small notice above the new door: 'Matilda Jenkyns, seller of tea'. Inside, the walls were white, and two great boxes of tea stood on the bare wooden floor. I spent my small savings on sweets for the children Miss Matty loved so much, and now her shop was ready to open.

Well, not quite. Miss Matty was worried because Mr Johnson also sold tea and she did not want to take business away from him. So she went down the street to talk to him about it. He was very kind to her, and I know that he sent her some of his own customers, by telling them that Miss Jenkyns's teas were better than the ones he sold. My businessman father shook his head. 'All very well in Cranford perhaps. You could not do business like that in Drumble!'

But I was delighted. Everyone suddenly seemed to need tea. Indeed, Miss Matty sold so much of it on the first two days that I felt able to leave her and go home to Drumble.

I returned every three months to check the shop and help Miss Matty with her business letters. This reminded me, of course, that no reply had ever come from India. I began to be ashamed of my letter to the Aga Jenkyns, and was glad I had told nobody about it.

About a year after Miss Matty opened her shop, Martha begged me to come back to Cranford. I went immediately in case Miss Matty was ill. She was not. When I looked quietly into the shop, there she was behind the table, happily knitting. The only problem was that Martha was expecting her first baby very soon, and Miss Matty did not realize it.

'I'm so afraid she won't approve!' cried Martha to me in

the kitchen. 'Will you tell her?'

I decided I would not. But a week later, I went in to see Miss Matty with a baby in my arms. She asked for her glasses, looked at it in surprise and was very silent all day. Then she went up to see Martha and they both cried with happiness. Shy, proud Jem shook my hand so hard that I still remember the pain.

While Martha was in bed, I was busy in the house. But sometimes I helped Miss Matty in the shop and was amused to watch her. She would never make a success of selling sweets! She gave away too many to every child who came in. But she had made more than £20 from selling tea in her first year, I discovered. She liked her new life, too, now that she was used to it. She met the country people, and they brought so many little presents of fruit and eggs for 'the old rector's daughter' that her table was sometimes quite full.

Cranford itself went on as usual. Mr and Mrs Hoggins were very happy together, though Mrs Jamieson still did not speak to them and even her man Mulliner avoided them in the street. It was now June. Martha was up again, and I was sitting in the shop one afternoon with Miss Matty when I saw a gentleman walk slowly past the window. He stood at the door, searching for a name. Then he came in. His hair was white, but his face was deep brown from the sun. It was the Aga Jenkyns, I knew it!

He stood opposite Miss Matty, just looking at her. Then he turned sharply to me. 'Is your name Mary Smith?'

'Yes!' I said.

'I've been too sudden for you, my little Matty,' Peter said.

He clearly did not know how to announce himself to Miss Matty, who was always shy when a man entered the shop. 'Give me a pound of those things,' he said, waving at some sweets.

'A pound!' Now Miss Matty looked up at him. 'Oh, sir! Can you be Peter?' she said, and trembled from head to foot.

In a moment, he was round the table and holding her in his arms. She was so white that I told Mr Peter to take her up to the drawing-room and put her on the sofa. 'I've been too sudden for you, my little Matty,' he said. She held her

brother's hand tightly and allowed him to carry her up. I left them to talk alone while I went down to tell a delighted Martha, and then back to the shop.

We had tea early that day. Miss Matty sat in the armchair opposite her brother, eating nothing, just looking at him. 'You were a boy when you left Cranford,' she said fondly, 'and now you have white hair!'

'And I forgot how time passes, Matty! I've brought you a pretty little dress from India! I remembered your taste. It was so like my dear mother's.'

At that name, the brother and sister held each other's hand even more tightly, and I got up to leave them together again. But Peter rose too. 'I must arrange for a room at the "George",' he said. 'My bag is there too.'

'No!' cried Miss Matty. 'Please, dear Peter, don't go! Mary, don't allow it!'

So I gave Mr Peter my room and moved in with Miss Matty. Poor Peter, she told me that night, had fought at Rangoon and been taken prisoner by the Burmese. Afterwards, his letters to England were returned with the word 'Dead' across them. So he had decided to stay out in the East as a planter. Then my letter arrived . . .

I do not think Peter came home from India a rich man, but a day or two later the shop was closed. The sweets were given to children, the tea was given to old people. The pretty dress was kept for Flora Gordon and, at about this time, many nice presents arrived for Miss Pole and Mrs Forrester, Mrs Fitz-Adam and Mrs Jamieson. I myself received handsome copies of Dr Johnson's books. Miss Matty begged me, with tears in her eyes, to consider them a present from her sister as well as herself.

Peter became a great favourite with the ladies of Cranford. He told 'wonderful stories' (though these stories were less wonderful, I noticed, when the rector was present). He had 'wonderful foreign ways' – he even sat on the floor at one of Miss Pole's parties. When Mrs Jamieson smiled her approval, I remembered she had once called Mr Hoggins 'vulgar' just because he crossed his legs as he sat on his chair.

So I returned to Drumble, leaving Miss Matty and Mr Peter very happy together. Martha and Jem remained willingly in the house, with baby Matilda. The only sadness was that Mrs Jamieson and the Hogginses were still not friends.

But then, one October morning, I received letters from Miss Pole and Miss Matty, asking me to come to Cranford. The dear Gordons were arriving on the fourteenth, they wrote, and had invited everyone to a lunch at the George Inn – even Miss Betty Barker, even Mr Hoggins and his wife, whom Major Gordon had met in Scotland.

Would Mrs Jamieson go to the lunch? When I arrived in Cranford, no one yet knew. Mr Peter, however, said she should and would go. 'Leave Mrs Jamieson to me,' he announced. The next thing we heard, from Miss Pole, was that Mrs Jamieson was indeed going.

Clever Mr Peter had arranged for 'Signor Brunoni, Conjurer to the King of Delhi' to return to Cranford Assembly Room 'in honour of the Honourable Mrs Jamieson'. Mrs Jamieson's name was written large on the notice. Mr Peter was sending everyone free tickets. And when was Signor Brunoni going to show his magic? On the evening of the Gordons' lunch . . .

So Mrs Jamieson came to the lunch, all smiles at Mr Peter's fantastic stories of his travels – and he entered the Assembly Room that evening with the Honourable Mrs Jamieson on one side and my lady, Mrs Hoggins, on the other.

71

Since that day, the old friendliness has returned to Cranford. I am pleased about this. My dear Miss Matty loves peace and kindness, and I think we are all better people when she is near.

GLOSSARY

Aga a title for an important man or leader in Muslim countries

announce to tell people some news, or that somebody has arrived

anxious worried and afraid

approve to consider someone or something acceptable; (*n*) **approval**

assembly people meeting together for a special purpose

beg to ask for something with strong feeling

bonnet a woman's hat, tied under the chin and worn outdoors

candle a stick of wax that gives light when it burns

cap a kind of soft hat of the times, worn by women indoors

carriage a wheeled vehicle for carrying people, pulled by horses

cart a vehicle for carrying things or people, pulled by a horse

conjurer a person who does clever tricks which seem magical

cough *(v)* to push out air violently and noisily through the throat

county *(n)* a district of Britain for local government purposes; (*adj*) having a high position in society

curtsy to bend at the knees with one foot in front of the other; done by women as a sign of respect

dimples small hollows in the cheeks or chin, made when smiling

drawing-room the 'best' room of a house, where guests are received

elder older of two members of a family (e.g. brothers or sisters)

estate a large area of land (not in a town) with one owner

fashion the latest, most popular way of dressing

forgive to stop being angry towards somebody or about something

funeral the ceremony of burying a dead person
gentleman a man of good family, often rich
honour great respect
Honourable a title for the children of some noblemen
in-law related by marriage
inn a public house or small old hotel
joke *(n)* something said or done to cause amusement or laughter
knit to make clothes out of wool, using long needles
landlady a woman who owns or manages a public house
late (of a person) not still alive, e.g. *my late father*
lodge to pay to live in someone's house
lord a title for some noblemen
love-affair a relationship between two people who are in love
magic making strange or mysterious things happen, which
    cannot easily be explained
maid a woman or a girl servant
marriage when a man and woman become husband and wife
mistress the woman in control of servants in a house
pillow a soft cushion for the head in a bed
poem a piece of writing in verse
rector a local priest in the Church of England
related in the same family
rent to make regular payments for living in someone else's house
respect *(n)* having a high opinion of someone and behaving with
    great politeness towards them
ribbon a long narrow piece of fine material for tying on clothes,
    round parcels, etc.
rule *(n)* what must or should be done (in polite society, in a
    school, when playing a game, etc.)
sermon the talk given by a priest during a church service

share *(n)* if you hold shares in a business company, you own
    small parts of it and receive payments if the business does well
shawl a large piece of material worn round a woman's shoulders
Signor the Italian word for 'sir' or 'Mr'
silk a fine, soft, natural material, usually smooth and shiny
society a class of people in a place who are of good family,
    important, fashionable, etc.
sofa a long comfortable seat with a back and sides
style a special way of doing something, e.g. writing or dressing
trade business; buying and selling, making something to sell
tray a flat piece of wood (or metal) for carrying food and
    drinks
trick *(n)* something clever or mysterious done to amuse people
turban a Muslim head-dress (a long piece of cloth tied round and
    round a man's head); also, a woman's hat which looks like this
twin a brother or sister born at the same time
vulgar not polite; not done by respectable people of good
    family
widow a woman whose husband is dead

Before Reading

1 Read the story introduction on the first page of the book, and the back cover. How much do you know now about life in Cranford? Are these sentences true (T) or false (F)?

1 Life in Cranford does not change very fast.
2 It is necessary to have a lot of food at parties.
3 Business people are an important part of Cranford society.
4 Talking about money is not considered polite.
5 The ladies of Cranford go to visit each other whenever they feel like it.
6 Although there are occasional arguments, the ladies of Cranford are usually good friends.

2 Can you guess what is going to happen in this story? Choose one answer for each question.

1 What will Miss Matty's happy surprise be?
   a) She is given a lot of money.
   b) A kind, handsome gentleman asks her to marry him.
   c) Someone she believed was dead comes home again.
   d) She opens a little shop, which is very successful.
2 Which of these sad things does not happen to Miss Matty?
   a) She loses nearly all her money.
   b) The ladies of Cranford stop visiting her.
   c) A man she loves dies.
   d) Her elder sister dies.

ACTIVITIES

While Reading

Read Chapters 1 to 3, then answer these questions.

1 How and why did the ladies' opinion of Captain Brown change?
2 What two things did Miss Jenkyns dislike about Miss Jessie?
3 What did Captain Brown and Miss Jenkyns disagree about?
4 How did Miss Jessie's life change after her father's death?
5 Why didn't Miss Matty marry Thomas Holbrook?
6 How did Miss Matty feel about Mr Holbrook during and after the visit, and how did Mary Smith know this?
7 Why do you think Miss Matty changed her mind about a follower for Martha after Mr Holbrook died?

Before you read Chapter 4 (*Poor Peter*), can you guess the answers to these questions?

1 Who was Peter?
   a) Miss Matty's brother.   c) Miss Matty's uncle.
   b) Miss Matty's cousin.   d) A man Miss Matty loved.
2 Why was he called 'poor Peter'?
   a) He was always ill.   c) He was always in trouble.
   b) He had no money.   d) He was always unhappy.
3 Where was Peter now?
   a) In London.   c) In Australia.
   b) In Scotland.   d) In India.

Read Chapters 4 and 5. Are these sentences true (T) or false (F)? Rewrite the false ones with the correct information.

1 Peter was a kind boy, but he was always playing jokes.
2 Peter locked himself in his room because his father had laughed at him in front of a crowd of people.
3 Peter wrote to his sister, begging her to send him money.
4 Deborah told Miss Matty that she had refused a hundred offers of marriage.
5 Miss Barker invited the ladies in order of their importance in Cranford society – which was Miss Pole, Miss Matty, Mrs Fitz-Adam, Mrs Jamieson, and finally, Mrs Forrester.
6 At Miss Barker's party the ladies ate a lot more than usual.
7 The ladies met Lady Glenmire as soon as she arrived.
8 Lady Glenmire was a nicer person than her sister-in-law.

Read Chapters 6 and 7. Choose the best question-word for these questions, and then answer them.

How / What / Who / Why

1 . . . did the ladies have a lot of questions for Miss Pole?
2 . . . was Miss Matty worried about watching magic tricks?
3 . . . helped Signor Brunoni and his family, and how?
4 . . . had helped the conjurer's wife when Phoebe was ill?
5 . . . news about Lady Glenmire surprised everybody?
6 . . . did Miss Matty give Mr Dobson five pound coins and take his note?
7 . . . happened to Miss Matty when her bank failed?
8 . . . did Mary Smith decide to do?

Before you read Chapters 8 and 9, can you guess who Miss Matty's 'true friends' were, and what they did? Choose some names and match them with the actions below.

Mary Smith and her father   Mrs Jamieson   Mrs Fitz-Adam
Signor Brunoni's wife   Miss Pole   Mr Hoggins
Martha and Jem Hearn   Mrs Forrester   Mr Johnson

1 . . . helped her to open a shop.
2 . . . sent customers to her shop.
3 . . . took her into their house as their lodger.
4 . . . offered to be her doctor for nothing.
5 . . . secretly gave her money.
6 . . . helped her to manage her business.

Read Chapters 8 and 9. Who said this, and to whom? Who, or what, were they talking about?

1 'I'll never leave her! I won't!'
2 'You stupid great thing! Why don't you speak?'
3 'It's just that a man needs time!'
4 'Miss Matty will think about your plan.'
5 'I wish it was more, my dear Mary. Indeed, I do!'
6 '. . . a gentleman rode beside her and was talking to her.'
7 'I could write a sermon about it if I was the rector!'
8 'You could not do business like that in Drumble!'
9 'I'm so afraid she won't approve!'
10 'I've been too sudden for you, . . .'
11 '. . . and now you have white hair!'
12 'Leave Mrs Jamieson to me.'

After Reading

1 Here are eight pieces of important Cranford news. Look at the replies, decide what the news is, and complete what the speaker is saying. (Use as many words as you like.) Then put the pieces of news in the right order for the story.

1 'My dear, have you heard the news? _____'
'How exciting! I wonder what he'll do. Perhaps he'll make things disappear – I've always wanted to see that.'

2 'I have some very sad news. Last night _____'
'Yes, we shall miss her very much. She always knew exactly what to do, and what the rules were.'

3 'My dear, you'll never believe this! _____'
'But that's extraordinary! Can it *really* be true? First a lord, and then – a doctor! Whatever will Mrs Jamieson say?'

4 'Something so exciting has happened! _____'
'That's wonderful! She must be so pleased. And all this time everybody thought that he was dead . . .'

5 'I've just seen a man in the street. He says _____'
'Oh, how terrible! Such a kind man – always thinking of other people first. And those two poor girls of his . . .'

6 'Have you heard? _____'
'No! Surely it's just a bit of fun. Have they looked everywhere? He'll be back soon, I'm sure.'

7 'Have you heard the news? _____'
   'The poor dear thing! To lose everything like that . . . Well, we must all think what we can do to help her.'

8 'I heard this from Miss Jenkyns herself. _____'
   'Going to be married? Oh, that's lovely news! I always said she had very pretty dimples.'

2 **What did Mary Smith say in her letter to the Aga Jenkyns (page 55)? Put the parts of sentences in the right order, and join them with these linking words to make four sentences.**

and / because / but / but when / if / which / who / who

Dear Mr Jenkyns,

1 _____ is a very dear friend of mine.
2 I felt sure you must be Miss Matty's missing brother.
3 _____ has suddenly failed,
4 _____ her brother would be able to do so much more.
5 I am writing to you about Miss Matilda Jenkyns,
6 _____ you are, your sister Miss Matty needs your help,
7 _____ Mrs Samuel Brown told me about the Aga Jenkyns,
8 We are doing what we can to help her,
9 _____ all her money was held in shares in a bank
10 Miss Matty believes that her brother Peter died in India,
11 _____ had helped to save her baby in Chunderabaddad,
12 _____ Miss Matty has lost almost everything.
Yours sincerely,
Mary Smith

3 Here are parts of letters written by characters in the story. Choose the best words (one for each gap) to complete them. Then say who wrote each letter, who received it, and what was happening at that point in the story.

1 I have some news _____ you, my dear, which _____ surprise you. I am _____ to be married to _____ Hoggins. He is such _____ kind and generous man! _____ is a very good _____ too, which I discovered _____ we were both helping _____ poor conjurer and his _____.

   I hope you are _____ your stay in Cheltenham . . .

2 I have some important _____ to discuss with you _____ our other friends. Please _____ sure to come to _____ house at eleven o'clock, _____ we cannot do anything _____ your help. Do not _____ the meeting or this _____ to *anyone* – this is _____ important.

3 I am _____ to invite you and _____ Smith to visit me _____ my little house here _____ Woodley next Tuesday. It _____ give me great pleasure _____ you would come to _____ and spend the day _____. I have asked my _____ Miss Pole too, so _____ three of you can _____ in the same carriage . . .

4 Your son Peter Jenkyns, _____ has just joined my _____, is a fine boy _____ I am sure he _____ make a good sailor. _____ the moment the ship _____ in the River Mersey, _____ we will sail south _____ the next few days. _____ you wish to see _____ son, you must come _____ once to Liverpool . . .

5 I am writing to _____ you to come back _____ Cranford.
We have a _____, and I don't know _____ to do. You are
_____ only person who can _____ Jem and me, and _____
must do something soon, _____ it will be too _____ . . .

6 There are worrying reports _____ the Town and County
_____. I warned Miss Jenkyns _____ ago not to buy _____
in this bank, but _____ did not take my _____. I hope Miss
Matty _____ not still have these _____, because they'll be
worth _____ if the bank fails . . .

4 Imagine that you are a reporter for the local newspaper in
Cranford. Write a report of the death of Captain Brown, using
these notes to help you.

• terrible accident / railway station
• captain reading / girl on line / train coming
• saved child / fell / under train
• Cranford two years / working for railway / two daughters
• popular and respected / greatly missed

5 What did you think about this story and its characters?
Complete some of these sentences.

1 I liked _____ *best/least* because _____.
2 The part of the story I enjoyed *most/least* was _____.
3 I *would/wouldn't* like _____ as a neighbour because

_____.

4 I *would/wouldn't* like to live in a small town like Cranford
because _____.

ABOUT THE AUTHOR

Elizabeth Gaskell was born Elizabeth Stevenson in London in 1810. After her mother's death, she went to live with her aunt in Knutsford, a quiet, old-fashioned country town (which became 'Cranford' in her novel). She had a good education, and in 1832 she married William Gaskell, a minister in the church.

The Gaskells went to live in Manchester ('Drumble' in the novel), a city which Mrs Gaskell both loved and hated – 'dear old dull ugly smoky grim grey Manchester', she called it. The Gaskells had five children, four daughters and a son, who died before he was a year old. Trying to forget this sadness, Mrs Gaskell wrote her first novel, *Mary Barton*, a story of the hard lives of factory workers in a big city. It was published in 1848 and was an immediate success, bringing Mrs Gaskell new friends, such as Charles Dickens and Charlotte Brontë. The very popular *Cranford* stories were first published in Dickens' magazine *Household Words*, and appeared as a book in 1853. Other novels followed, including *Ruth* (1853), *North and South* (1855), *Cousin Phillis* (1864), and *Wives and Daughters*, which was left unfinished when Mrs Gaskell died suddenly in 1865.

Mrs Gaskell is also famous for her biography of her friend Charlotte Brontë, published two years after Charlotte's death in 1855, and still recognized as one of the great biographies. From the novels, *Cranford* was and remains a great favourite with many readers, for its gentle humour and amusing pictures of small-town life. Mrs Gaskell herself said of it: 'It is the only one of my own books that I can read again; but whenever I am ill, I take *Cranford* and . . . laugh over it.'

OXFORD BOOKWORMS LIBRARY

Classics • Crime & Mystery • Factfiles • Fantasy & Horror
Human Interest • Playscripts • Thriller & Adventure
True Stories • World Stories

The OXFORD BOOKWORMS LIBRARY provides enjoyable reading in English, with a wide range of classic and modern fiction, non-fiction, and plays. It includes original and adapted texts in seven carefully graded language stages, which take learners from beginner to advanced level. An overview is given on the next pages.

All Stage 1 titles are available as audio recordings, as well as over eighty other titles from Starter to Stage 6. All Starters and many titles at Stages 1 to 4 are specially recommended for younger learners. Every Bookworm is illustrated, and Starters and Factfiles have full-colour illustrations.

The OXFORD BOOKWORMS LIBRARY also offers extensive support. Each book contains an introduction to the story, notes about the author, a glossary, and activities. Additional resources include tests and worksheets, and answers for these and for the activities in the books. There is advice on running a class library, using audio recordings, and the many ways of using Oxford Bookworms in reading programmes. Resource materials are available on the website <www.oup.com/elt/bookworms>.

The *Oxford Bookworms Collection* is a series for advanced learners. It consists of volumes of short stories by well-known authors, both classic and modern. Texts are not abridged or adapted in any way, but carefully selected to be accessible to the advanced student.

You can find details and a full list of titles in the *Oxford Bookworms Library Catalogue* and *Oxford English Language Teaching Catalogues*, and on the website <www.oup.com/elt/bookworms>.

THE OXFORD BOOKWORMS LIBRARY
GRADING AND SAMPLE EXTRACTS

STARTER • 250 HEADWORDS

present simple – present continuous – imperative –
can/cannot, must – going to (future) – simple gerunds ...

Her phone is ringing – but where is it?

Sally gets out of bed and looks in her bag. No phone. She looks under the bed. No phone. Then she looks behind the door. There is her phone. Sally picks up her phone and answers it. *Sally's Phone*

STAGE 1 • 400 HEADWORDS

... past simple – coordination with *and*, *but*, *or* –
subordination with *before*, *after*, *when*, *because*, *so* ...

I knew him in Persia. He was a famous builder and I worked with him there. For a time I was his friend, but not for long. When he came to Paris, I came after him – I wanted to watch him. He was a very clever, very dangerous man. *The Phantom of the Opera*

STAGE 2 • 700 HEADWORDS

... present perfect – *will* (future) – *(don't) have to, must not, could* –
comparison of adjectives – simple *if* clauses – past continuous –
tag questions – *ask/tell* + infinitive ...

While I was writing these words in my diary, I decided what to do. I must try to escape. I shall try to get down the wall outside. The window is high above the ground, but I have to try. I shall take some of the gold with me – if I escape, perhaps it will be helpful later. *Dracula*

STAGE 3 • 1000 HEADWORDS

... should, may – present perfect continuous – *used to* – past perfect –
causative – relative clauses – indirect statements ...

Of course, it was most important that no one should see
Colin, Mary, or Dickon entering the secret garden. So Colin
gave orders to the gardeners that they must all keep away
from that part of the garden in future. *The Secret Garden*

STAGE 4 • 1400 HEADWORDS

... past perfect continuous – passive (simple forms) –
would conditional clauses – indirect questions –
relatives with *where/when* – gerunds after prepositions/phrases ...

I was glad. Now Hyde could not show his face to the world
again. If he did, every honest man in London would be proud
to report him to the police. *Dr Jekyll and Mr Hyde*

STAGE 5 • 1800 HEADWORDS

... future continuous – future perfect –
passive (modals, continuous forms) –
would have conditional clauses – modals + perfect infinitive ...

If he had spoken Estella's name, I would have hit him. I was so
angry with him, and so depressed about my future, that I could
not eat the breakfast. Instead I went straight to the old house.
Great Expectations

STAGE 6 • 2500 HEADWORDS

... passive (infinitives, gerunds) – advanced modal meanings –
clauses of concession, condition

When I stepped up to the piano, I was confident. It was as if I
knew that the prodigy side of me really did exist. And when I
started to play, I was so caught up in how lovely I looked that
I didn't worry how I would sound. *The Joy Luck Club*

Persuasion

JANE AUSTEN

Retold by Clare West

At nineteen Anne Elliot refuses an offer of marriage from Frederick Wentworth, persuaded to do so by Lady Russell, a friend of her dead mother. Wentworth is a sailor, with no money and an uncertain future, says Lady Russell – just a nobody, certainly not worthy of a baronet's daughter.

Eight years later Wentworth returns, a rich and successful captain, looking for a wife. Anne is still unmarried, but Captain Wentworth clearly prefers the company of the two Musgrove girls . . .

Jane Austen's tale of love and marriage is told with humour and a sharp understanding of human behaviour.

Little Women

LOUISA MAY ALCOTT

Retold by John Escott

When Christmas comes for the four March girls, there is no money for expensive presents and they give away their Christmas breakfast to a poor family. But there are no happier girls in America than Meg, Jo, Beth, and Amy. They miss their father, of course, who is away at the Civil War, but they try hard to be good so that he will be proud of his 'little women' when he comes home.

This heart-warming story of family life has been popular for more than a hundred years.